Under the Sea
Lobsters

by Jody Sullivan Rake

Consulting Editor: Gail Saunders-Smith, PhD

Consultant: Debbie Nuzzolo
Education Manager
SeaWorld, San Diego, California

Capstone
press®

Mankato, Minnesota

Pebble Plus is published by Capstone Press,
151 Good Counsel Drive, P.O. Box 669, Mankato, Minnesota 56002.
www.capstonepress.com

1 2 3 4 5 6 11 10 09 08 07 06

Library of Congress Cataloging-in-Publication Data
Rake, Jody Sullivan.
    Lobsters / by Jody Sullivan Rake.
    p. cm.—(Pebble Plus. Under the sea)
    Summary: "Simple text and photographs describe the lives of lobsters"—Provided by publisher.
    Includes bibliographical references and index.
    ISBN-13: 978-0-7368-6363-6 (hardcover)
    ISBN-10: 0-7368-6363-X (hardcover)
    1. Lobsters—Juvenile literature. I. Title. II. Series: Under the sea (Mankato, Minn.)
QL444.M33 R35 2007
595.3'84—dc22   2005036010

Editorial Credits
Mari Schuh, editor; Juliette Peters, set designer; Patrick D. Dentinger, book designer; Kelly Garvin,
        photo researcher/photo editor

Photo Credits
Corbis/Stephen Frink, 7
Herb Segars, 14–15
Jeff Rotman/Doug Perrine, 21
PhotoDisc Inc., back cover
Seapics/Andrew J. Martinez, cover, 5; David B. Fleetham, 1; Doug Perrine, 9, 10–11; Espen Rekdal, 17;
        Jonathan Bird, 12–13; Michele Hall, 18–19

Note to Parents and Teachers

The Under the Sea set supports national science standards related to the evolution of
life. This book describes and illustrates lobsters. The images support early readers in
understanding the text. The repetition of words and phrases helps early readers learn
new words. This book also introduces early readers to subject-specific vocabulary words,
which are defined in the Glossary section. Early readers may need assistance to read
some words and to use the Table of Contents, Glossary, Read More, Internet Sites, and
Index sections of the book.

Table of Contents

What Are Lobsters?. 4
Body Parts. 8
What Lobsters Do 14
Under the Sea. 20

Glossary 22
Read More 23
Internet Sites. 23
Index 24

What Are Lobsters?

Lobsters are ocean animals.

They live on the ocean floor.

Lobsters keep growing

their whole life.

Most lobsters are

about the size

of an adult's foot.

Body Parts

Lobsters have hard shells.

Eight legs stick out

from a lobster's body.

Two long antennas
reach out from
a lobster's head.
Lobsters feel and smell
for food with their antennas.

Some lobsters catch food
with claws called pincers.
They also fight predators
and other lobsters
with their pincers.

What Lobsters Do

A female lobster carries
thousands of eggs
under her tail.
The eggs stick to her.

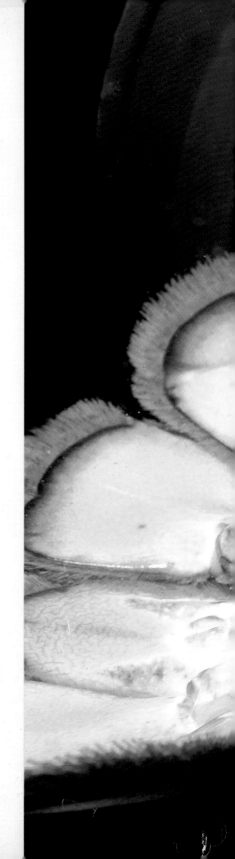

Young lobsters hatch.

They float freely

for a few weeks.

Then they move down

to the ocean floor.

Lobsters shed
their hard shells
as they grow.
Their soft bodies then
harden into new shells.

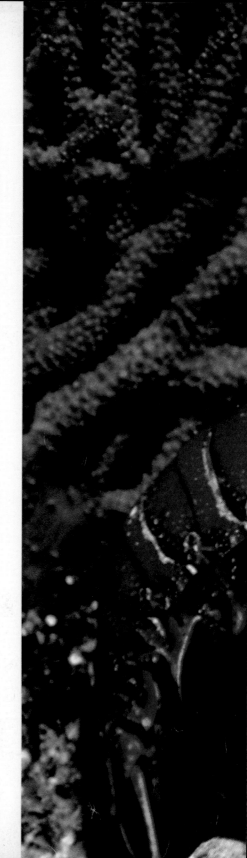

Under the Sea

Under the sea,

lobsters walk along

the ocean floor.

Glossary

antenna—a feeler on an animal's head; animals use antennas to smell and feel.

pincers—pinching claws; many ocean animals use their pincers to catch food, eat, and fight.

predator—an animal that hunts and eats other animals

shed—to get rid of; lobsters shed their shells when they grow.

shell—a hard protective covering on the outside of some animals

Read More

Gilpin, Daniel. *Lobsters, Crabs, and Other Crustaceans.* Animal Kingdom Classification. Minneapolis: Compass Point Books, 2006.

Lassieur, Allison. *Crabs, Lobsters, and Shrimps.* Animals in Order. New York: Franklin Watts, 2003.

Schaefer, Lola M. *Lobsters.* Musty-Crusty Animals. Chicago: Heinemann, 2002.

Internet Sites

FactHound offers a safe, fun way to find Internet sites related to this book. All of the sites on FactHound have been researched by our staff.

Here's how:

1. Visit *www.facthound.com*

2. Choose your grade level.

3. Type in this book ID **073686363X** for age-appropriate sites. You may also browse subjects by clicking on letters, or by clicking on pictures and words.

4. Click on the **Fetch It** button.

FactHound will fetch the best sites for you!

Index

antennas, 10

eggs, 14

females, 14

fighting, 12

food, 10, 12

growing, 6, 18

hatching, 16

legs, 8

ocean floor, 4, 16, 20

pincers, 12

predators, 12

shedding, 18

shells, 8, 18

size, 6

smelling, 10

tails, 14

walking, 20

young lobsters, 16

Word Count: 132
Grade: 1
Early-Intervention Level: 14